Out and About at CITY HALL

by Nancy Garhan Attebury
illustrated by Zachary Trover

Special thanks to our advisers for their expertise:

Merry L. Keefe, City Clerk
Minneapolis, Minnesota

Susan Kesselring, M.A., Literacy Educator
Rosemount–Apple Valley–Eagan (Minnesota) School District

PICTURE WINDOW BOOKS
Minneapolis, Minnesota

The author wishes to thank the Attebury family, City Recorder Gary Fletcher, Susan Blackaby, and Robin Michal Koontz.

Editorial Director: Carol Jones
Managing Editor: Catherine Neitge
Creative Director: Keith Griffin
Editor: Jill Kalz
Story Consultant: Terry Flaherty
Designer: Zachary Trover
Page Production: Picture Window Books
The illustrations in this book were created digitally.

Picture Window Books
5115 Excelsior Boulevard
Suite 232
Minneapolis, MN 55416
877-845-8392
www.picturewindowbooks.com

Printed in the United States of America.

Library of Congress Cataloging-in-Publication Data
Attebury, Nancy Garhan.
Out and about at city hall / by Nancy Garhan Attebury ; illustrated by Zachary Trover.
p. cm. — (Field trips)
Includes bibliographical references and index.
ISBN 1-4048-1146-X (hardcover)
1. Municipal government—United States—Juvenile literature. I. Trover, Zachary. II. Title.
III. Field trips (Picture Window Books)
JS331.G37 2006
320.8'5'0973—dc22   2005004262

We're going on a field trip to city hall. We can't wait!

Things to find out:

Who works at city hall?

What kinds of plans are made at city hall?

What are public utilities?

What does the mayor do?

3

Good morning! My name is Penny, and I'm the Rushford city manager. I work here at city hall.

What do you think makes a city a good place to live? Parks? A lot of stores and restaurants? Those things are important, but a city also needs good roads, police and fire protection, and much more.

A city manager oversees many city workers. Four years of college are needed for the job. He or she needs to be very organized and willing to be a leader.

My job as the city manager is to make sure people in Rushford have all the basic things they need. Clean water, sewer service, and garbage pick-up are just some of those needs.

I also schedule fun public activities, such as parades and picnics. On the wall is a picture from last year's Fourth of July celebration.

The city is responsible for the disposal of its citizens' sewage. Sewer pipes run from each building to larger pipes beneath city streets. These larger pipes carry sewage to a wastewater treatment plant, where the water is cleaned and disinfected.

The City of Rushford

SERVICES	WHO PROVIDES THEM
Water and Sewer	Water Department
Garbage	Sanitation Department, Recycling Center
Streets and Roads	Road Department
Fire Protection	Fire Department
Health Care	Public Health Nurse and Staff
Law Enforcement	Police Department
Transportation	Department of Transportation

This chart shows some of the services Rushford provides. Bigger cities may offer more services, and smaller cities may offer less. Some cities, for example, have a parks and recreation department. That department takes care of the city parks, ice rinks, swimming pools, and athletic fields.

City records are saved on computers. Some records show things such as who paid their water bill or who owns a piece of land. Other records show how much city workers are paid or where underground sewer pipes lie.

People who own homes and businesses in the city pay taxes for city services. These services include police and fire protection, road care, public transportation, libraries, and animal control.

Other city services, such as water and sewer, are called public utilities. Each month, citizens receive a public utility bill from the city. They can mail their payment, drop it off here at the cashier window, or pay online.

DEPOSIT

CITY HALL

TAKE ONE

In some cities, private companies provide utilities. In these cities, citizens can choose which company they want.

Have you ever ridden on a city bus? At city hall we have maps of bus routes. The bus system is one of many kinds of public transportation. Anybody may use it, but there is a fee to ride.

Kids your age can buy a student pass that is good for many rides, or you can pay each time you ride. You could ride to the library or swimming pool on a city bus. Light rail systems (also called streetcars or city trains) and subways are two other kinds of public transportation.

A bus schedule shows the time a bus arrives at a bus stop. It also shows what time it leaves the stop. A bus map shows different routes. The routes are shown in different colors. Most city buses cover the same routes every day.

Ideas for City Funding:

Library improvements	$140,000
New science museum	$257,000
New parking meters	$10,000
Bike trail	$13,750

The city council meets in this big room. Adult citizens vote to elect the council members. Each council member represents, or speaks for, a different part of the city and the citizens who live there.

Every year the council studies the city budget. This is the money used to run the city. The council listens to what the citizens want, decides what projects to fund, and then figures out how to pay for them.

In addition to paying taxes directly to the city, people pay an extra tax when they put gas in their cars. Those tax dollars go to the state government first, then some of the money is given back to the cities. That money goes into a general fund to help pay for services managed from city hall.

This is Gary, our city recorder. He keeps a written record of what happens in city council meetings. These notes are called minutes.

CITY RECORDER

For example, the city council may vote on where to put a new park. Gary writes down what the council members said and how they voted.

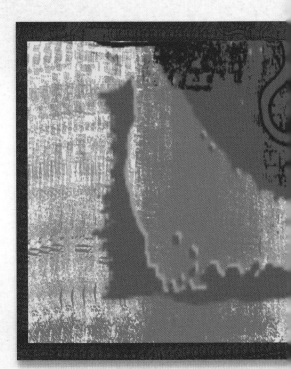

A city also makes money from a variety of fees. Money collected from parking meters, fines, and the sale of permits and licenses are added to the city budget.

Right next to Gary is the mayor's office. Mayor Perez works at city hall, too. She leads our city government. The city government decides how the city will do things.

The city government works with county and state governments to make sure city projects are safe for people and the environment. Mayor Perez attends many public events. She talks to as many people as she can so she has a better understanding of the citizens she represents.

Adults in a city vote to elect the mayor. Several people may want the job. Voters choose a mayor who thinks like them and can do what they want. A mayor supports projects that will make the city a good place to live.

It's important to know how your city works. It's also important for you to let us know how we can make Rushford an even better place for everyone. Thanks for visiting city hall today!

PLANNING YOUR OWN CITY

Pretend you work at city hall. It's your job to plan where things will go in your city.

What you need:

a ruler and a yardstick

a pencil

a large sheet of blank chart paper

10 pieces of paper about the size of gum wrappers

colored markers

tape

What you do:

1. Use the yardstick to draw lines on the paper like this:

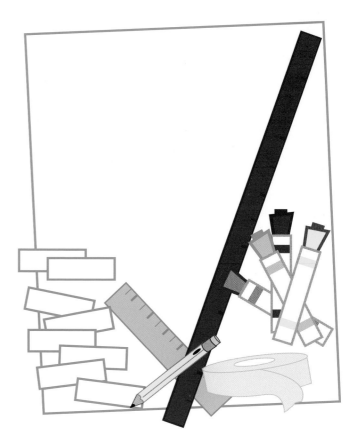

2. Using the following list, write a different word on each of the 10 small pieces of paper: Library, Park, Recycling Center, Fire Station, My House, Police Station, City Hall, Airport, Bus Station, School. You may want to draw a small picture of each place, too.

3. Write "City Plan" on the top of the chart paper. Pretend the large paper shows one whole city.

4. Pick up the small paper that says "City Hall." Decide where you want to put it in your city, and tape it in place.

5. Move the other small pieces where you want them in your city. Plan carefully. Do you really want to put the noisy airport by the library? Where is the best place to put a bus station? When you're done, tape the pieces in place.

6. Use the pencil and ruler to draw streets. Make up names for the streets, and label them.

7. Use a colored marker to show bus routes. Add bus stops, too.

8. When your city is complete, hang up your city plan for other people to enjoy. Would they want to live in your city? Why or why not?

FUN FACTS

- A city's flag and official seal can be found at city hall. The flag and seal are a traditional part of U.S. cities. People, animals, plants, words, and dates may be found on a city's flag and seal.

- A city's transportation department does more than manage city buses and trains. It also takes care of parking meters, streetlights, and even city bridges.

- Animal control is a city service. Animal control officers pick up stray animals and take them to shelters, where they can be claimed by their owners or adopted. Shelters in the United States care for more than six million dogs and cats each year. Officers also trap troublesome animals, such as raccoons or snakes, near people's homes and let them go outside the city limits.

- The New York City Fire Department is the largest fire department in the United States. About 11,500 firefighters protect more than eight million citizens.

GLOSSARY

council—a group of people elected to make decisions for a larger group

fund—to pay for; money put aside for something special is also called a fund

manage—to take care of and keep running smoothly

mayor—the leader of city government

minutes—written notes that tell what took place at a meeting

permits—written permissions to do something; examples include hunting, fishing, and building permits

projects—specific plans

record—a collection of facts

schedule—a timetable telling when things will happen

services—acts that help people

TO LEARN MORE

At the Library

DeGezelle, Terri. *The City Mayor*. Mankato, Minn.: Capstone Press, 2005.

Flanagan, Alice K. *Mayors*. Minneapolis: Compass Point Books, 2001.

Giesecke, Ernestine. *Local Government*. Chicago: Heinemann Library, 2000.

On the Web

FactHound offers a safe, fun way to find Web sites related to this book. All of the sites on FactHound have been researched by our staff. *www.facthound.com*

1. Visit the FactHound home page.
2. Enter a search word related to this book, or type in this special code: 140481146X.
3. Click on the FETCH IT button.

Your trusty FactHound will fetch the best sites for you!

Look for all the books in the Field Trips series:

Out and About at ...
The Apple Orchard
The Aquarium
The Bakery
The Bank
City Hall
The Dairy Farm
The Fire Station
The Hospital
The Newspaper
The Orchestra
The Planetarium
The Post Office
The Public Library
The Science Center
The Supermarket
The United States Mint
The Vet Clinic
The Zoo